D1301001

ANIMALS ON THE BRINK

Gorillas

Patricia Miller-Schroeder

www.av2books.com

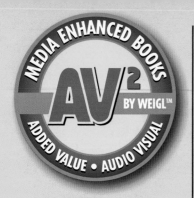

AV² provides enriched content that supplements and complements this book. Weigl's AV² books strive to create inspired learning and engage young minds in a total learning experience.

Your AV² Media Enhanced books come alive with...

Audio
Listen to sections of the book read aloud.

Key Words
Study vocabulary, and complete a matching word activity.

Video
Watch informative video clips.

Quizzes
Test your knowledge.

Embedded Weblinks
Gain additional information for research.

Slide Show
View images and captions, and prepare a presentation.

Try This!
Complete activities and hands-on experiments.

... and much, much more!

Go to **www.av2books.com**, and enter this book's unique code.

BOOK CODE

A 1 8 8 1 4 7

AV² by Weigl brings you media enhanced books that support active learning.

Published by AV² by Weigl
350 5th Avenue, 59th Floor
New York, NY 10118
Website: www.av2books.com   www.weigl.com

Library of Congress Cataloguing in Publication data available upon request.
Fax 1-866-449-3445 for the attention of the Publishing Records department.

ISBN 978-1-61913-425-6 (hard cover)
ISBN 978-1-61913-426-3 (soft cover)

Printed in the United States of America in North Mankato, Minnesota
1 2 3 4 5 6 7 8 9 16 15 14 13 12

052012
WEP170512

Project Coordinator Aaron Carr
Design Mandy Christiansen

Every reasonable effort has been made to trace ownership and to obtain permission to reprint copyright material. The publishers would be pleased to have any errors or omissions brought to their attention so that they may be corrected in subsequent printings.

Photo Credits
Weigl acknowledges Getty Images as its primary photo supplier for this title.

Contents

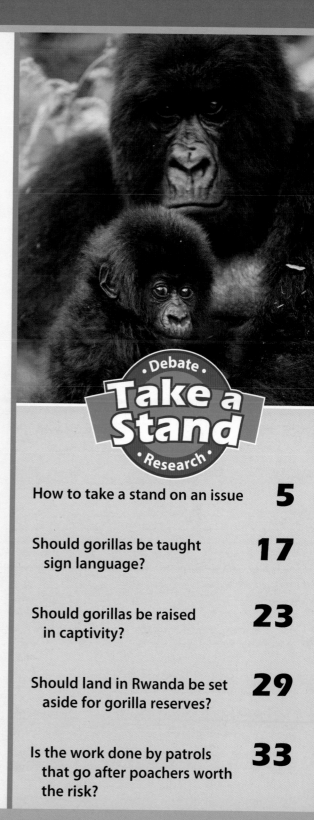

Take a Stand
Debate · Research

The Gorilla

People have long been fascinated by gorillas. The Europeans who first saw gorillas in Africa brought back stories about fierce black apes. In books and movies, the apes were portrayed as monsters. Many people feared the gorilla's size and strength. Others mistook the gorilla's calm nature for dullness.

To understand the gorilla's true nature, turn the pages. In this book, you will read about the importance of a gorilla group leader. You will learn what it means when a gorilla beats its chest. You will discover what scares gorillas and find out what these gentle creatures are really like.

Gorillas have been portrayed as fearsome, but these large animals naturally stay to themselves in the forest.

Gorillas grow 32 teeth, which is the same number of permanent teeth that most humans have.

How to Take a Stand on an Issue

Research is important to the study of any scientific field. When scientists choose a subject to study, they must conduct research to ensure they have a thorough understanding of the topic. They ask questions about the subject and then search for answers. Sometimes, however, there is no clear answer to a question. In these cases, scientists must use the information they have to form a hypothesis, or theory. They must take a stand on one side of an issue or the other. Follow the process below for each Take a Stand section in this book to determine where you stand on these issues.

1. **What Is the Issue?**
   a. Determine a research subject, and form a general question about the subject.

2. **Form a Hypothesis**
   a. Search at the library and online for sources of information on the subject.
   b. Conduct basic research on the subject to narrow down the general question.
   c. Form a hypothesis on the subject based on research to this point.
   d. Make predictions based on the hypothesis. What are the expected results?

3. **Research the Issue**
   a. Conduct extensive research using a variety of sources, including books, scientific journals, and reliable websites.
   b. Collect data on the issue and take notes on all information gathered from research.
   c. Draw conclusions based on the information collected.

4. **Conclusion**
   a. Explain the research findings.
   b. Was the hypothesis proved or disproved?

Guide to Gorillas

In nature, gorillas can live for 35 to 45 years, but like other animals, many gorillas die young. Some scientists estimate that 35 to 40 percent of gorillas in nature die when young. Many gorilla deaths are the result of accidents, disease, or hunters. Gorillas have lived to age 55 in captivity.

Newborn gorillas weigh about half as much as newborn humans. Baby gorillas learn to crawl at about 2 months old.

Features

In a Florida zoo, a baby gorilla used to attract crowds by beating her chest. She would imitate her father to delight her parents. To the people watching, the gorillas' actions seemed almost human. It was clear that the little gorilla was her "daddy's girl."

Genetic evidence shows that humans and gorillas are similar but different. Both are part of the **order** of animals called **primates**. The gorilla is in the great ape **family**, which also includes chimpanzees. Great apes are often mistaken for the primates known as monkeys, but none of the great apes have tails, and most monkeys have tails.

Male gorillas typically weigh 300 to 400 pounds (135 to 180 kilograms), though some are even heavier. Adult females usually range from 150 to 250 pounds (68 to 113 kg). Adult males can be 5.5 to 6 feet (1.7 to 1.8 meters) tall, with an arm span from 7.5 to 8.5 feet (2.3 to 2.6 m). Female gorillas are shorter, with a smaller arm span. Males and females are similar in size until they are about 8 years old. By the time males are 12 years old, they weigh twice as much as females. Although gorillas spend a great deal of time resting and eating, they are not lazy. Their size and habits are adaptations to their forest environment and diet.

When gorillas are born, their skin is often pink or pinkish gray. Sometimes, it may be light brown. Some baby gorillas have pink spots on the soles of their feet and hands. As gorillas grow, their skin turns black on their face, ears, fingers, and chest. Their hair is mostly black. On some gorillas, it is a rich blue-black color. Other gorillas have hair with gray, brown, or red overtones. When a male gorilla is 11 or 12 years old, a saddle-shaped area of back hair turns a silver color. This means the male is old enough to lead a group and to mate. When males reach this age, they are called silverbacks. Younger male gorillas are called blackbacks. As gorillas age, the hair on their head and shoulders sometimes turns gray.

Classification

Gorillas belong to a large order of animals called primates. This order has 13 families and more than 230 living **species**. These species include different types of monkeys, apes, and a third group of animals on a different branch of the family tree.

There are two main groups of primates, called the prosimians and the anthropoids. The prosimians include the lemur and the tarsier. The anthropoids include the gorilla. Anthropoids are divided into New World and Old World branches. The New World group includes spider monkeys and howler monkeys. The Old World category includes the apes and many kinds of monkeys. The apes include lesser apes, such as the gibbon, and great apes, such as the gorilla.

Of all living primates, gorillas are the largest. The smallest primates are the pygmy mouse lemurs. These prosimian primates weigh only about 2 ounces (60 grams).

There are two species of gorilla living today in Africa. They are *Gorilla gorilla* and *Gorilla beringei*. Scientists divide the gorilla species into four subspecies. All look similar, but each subspecies has slightly different characteristics. Researchers are trying to determine whether a fifth subspecies is living in Uganda.

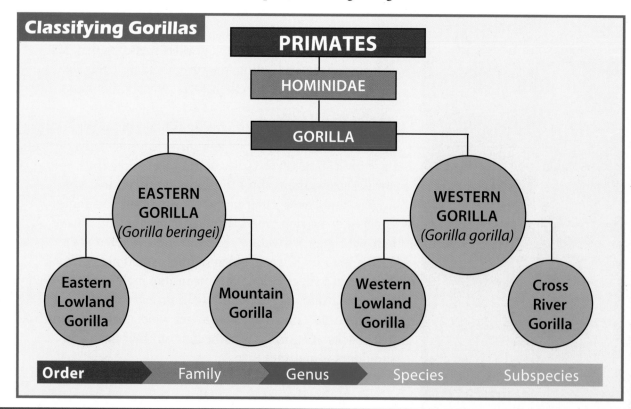

Classifying Gorillas

PRIMATES

HOMINIDAE

GORILLA

EASTERN GORILLA (*Gorilla beringei*)

WESTERN GORILLA (*Gorilla gorilla*)

Eastern Lowland Gorilla

Mountain Gorilla

Western Lowland Gorilla

Cross River Gorilla

Order → Family → Genus → Species → Subspecies

The western lowland gorilla, which has the scientific name *Gorilla gorilla gorilla*, is the most widespread subspecies. It lives in the tropical forests of West Africa. It is the shortest in height and lightest in weight.

The eastern lowland gorilla, or *Gorilla beringei graueri*, lives in rainforests in Central Africa. This subspecies is larger than the western lowland gorilla.

The mountain gorilla, or *Gorilla beringei beringei*, is the largest of gorillas. This subspecies lives in the cool, damp highlands of Rwanda.

Special Adaptations

A gorilla is a **herbivore** that spends most of the day eating or looking for food. The rest of its day is spent getting from place to place, socializing, or napping. Gorillas sleep during the night. They have many special features that help them survive in their natural environment.

Eyes

Gorillas have low foreheads, with bony ridges that stick out over their eyes for protection. Their eyes, which can see in color, are in front of their heads. This allows them to judge distance.

Nose

Gorillas rely on their sense of smell to warn them of danger. Each of the subspecies of gorillas has a different nose shape. Even within the same subspecies, noses can look quite different.

Hands

A gorilla's hands have four flexible fingers and an **opposable** thumb. Gorillas can use their fingers and thumb to pick up or hold objects, to pull off leaves and other parts from plants, and to pick small objects out of their hair. Like humans, gorillas have tiny raised ridges, or fingerprints, on the tips of their fingers. These ridges help gorillas feel objects.

Ears

The eardrums inside a gorilla's ears are the largest in the animal kingdom. The gorilla listens for signs of danger. Many people studying gorillas have noted that the human voice is the one sound that almost always causes gorillas to run away.

Teeth and Jaws

On the top of their heads, gorillas have a bony ridge called the **sagittal crest**. The crests are especially pronounced in males. The big muscles that move the jaw are attached to the sagittal crest. Gorilla jaws are made of thick, sturdy bone. Their molar teeth are broad and flat for grinding plant food. Males have large **canine** teeth that they display to scare rivals.

Feet

The gorilla's big toes are also opposable, which allows the gorilla to grasp objects with its feet.

Groups

Gorillas live in social groups that are in many ways like families. The group is very important to them. Living together is safer for gorillas. Group members can spot predators and give alarm calls. Mother gorillas caring for their young get help from other females. Many male gorillas also help protect and care for young ones. During the day, the group travels and feeds together. At night, group members sleep close together. In the group, young gorillas learn how to survive and get along with other gorillas. Even gorillas that live in zoos and animal parks are happier when they live in groups.

Gorilla groups usually have 5 to 20 members, although even larger groups are sometimes seen. The leader of each group is a large silverback male. There will be at least two adult females in a group. In addition to the silverback and females, a gorilla group will have infants and young gorillas. Most female offspring change groups when they become adults. Most males do as well. They wander alone or with other males until they can form their own group.

Life in a gorilla group is peaceful and friendly. Group members will nap with or groom one another during rest periods. Females will serve as "aunts" for one another's youngsters. There is rarely any fighting. The silverback can stop most squabbles by simply standing still and glaring at the troublemakers. This is a message to the other gorillas that they should behave themselves.

Gorillas are usually even-tempered and quiet. However, within each group, there will be some gorillas that are more nervous, calm, shy, or aggressive than others. The personality of the silverback affects all of the other gorillas in the group. The silverback is the group's decision-maker. Each day, he decides where the group will go to feed. He also decides when to travel to other areas and when to stop for the night. The silverback is also the main defender. When danger threatens, he will place himself between danger and the other members of his group.

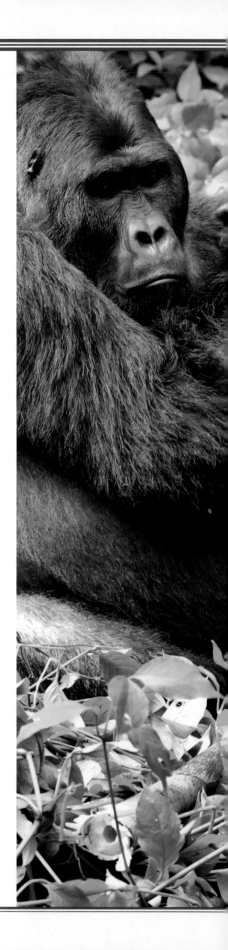

Young male outsiders sometimes challenge the silverback to see if he is able to defend his females. The weakest bonds are the bonds among females.

Gorilla groups are also known as troops. Some of the larger troops have been known to have as many as 30 members.

Guide to Gorillas

Some of the sounds gorillas make are similar to sounds made by other animals. Gorillas have a call like a cat's purr. Other calls sound like a dog's bark or a horse's neigh.

When a silverback roars, the group automatically hides behind him. The roar indicates some kind of threat.

Communication

Like people, gorillas sneeze, cough, yawn, hiccup, burp, and laugh. They also have at least 17 different **vocalizations**. Some are used more often than others. The most common is a belch that sounds like someone clearing his or her throat. When one animal gives a rumbling belch, it will be answered by others to show that they feel content. A sharp pig-grunt noise is a common sound that means the gorilla is annoyed. It might be heard when a mother scolds an infant or when a silverback stops a squabble. A hoot-bark sound shows curiosity or mild alarm. It is often used by the silverback to alert the group. A series of grunts may be used to keep group members together. Barks and screams are heard when gorillas fight. Gorillas will show their canine teeth and make loud noises when they are angry or when they want to scare off an intruder.

The male leaders from different groups give a special "hoo-hoo-hoo" series of calls when they are close to one another. These calls can be heard from as far away as a half-mile (0.8 kilometers). They are answered by the males of other groups. In this way, the groups can avoid one another.

When gorillas see humans, they make sounds like roars and screams to warn the group. When gorillas are very frightened and when danger is very close, they suddenly become quiet. The sudden silence tells the rest of the group that danger is near, without giving away the location of the group.

Gorillas use facial expressions and move their mouths in ways that are similar to humans. They will gaze with meaning at one another. They will also use sounds, such as hooting, grunting, and chuckling, to indicate feeling.

From an Expert

From 1991 to 1993, Dieter Steklis was director of the Karisoke Research Center in Rwanda, where he studied gorilla communication. He has edited or written many publications on primates.

"Virtually everyone who has worked with gorillas feels an indescribable sense of awe, mixed with fear, and yet feels trust and unmistakable community when in their presence." - Dieter Steklis

Body Language

On the ground, gorillas usually move by **knuckle-walking**. The gorilla's feet are flat on the ground, while most of its weight is carried on the backs of its fingers. If a gorilla walks upright, it is usually for short distances as a display of its size or strength. Gorillas are intelligent animals that use different displays, body language, and vocalizations to send messages to one another. There is some indication that their gestures vary from one group to another.

Excitement

The gorilla's chest-beating display starts with a series of hoots. The gorilla then rises on its hind legs, throws plants in the air, and kicks upward with one leg. Next, it beats its chest with its hands, making a loud "pok-pok-pok" sound. The gorilla then runs sideways, tearing up plants and slapping the ground. The display is sometimes done to scare others. It is also done to get attention or to relieve stress.

Submission

Gorillas have many ways of showing that they mean no harm. A gorilla may turn its head and face away from another animal. It may crouch down, lower its head, and tuck its arms and legs under its body. This submissive behavior will usually stop aggression. Just as with humans, staring directly at a gorilla for a long time may cause it to feel threatened or uncomfortable.

Aggression

To show aggression, a silverback may turn sideways and yawn to show his big teeth. When gorillas shake their heads, it means a display is coming. To show anger, a gorilla may stare, turn its head sharply, lunge, or bluff charge. In a bluff charge, one gorilla runs toward another, but stops a few feet away. If this does not work, the gorilla may wrestle with or bite the other gorilla. It is rare for aggressive behavior to go past a stare or a lunge.

Closeness

Gorillas will groom one another to foster a sense of belonging. Mothers clean up the infants. Males groom females as part of the mating ritual. Most often, the gorilla that does the grooming is trying to be friendly with the gorilla being groomed. Gorillas huddle to show closeness with friends and family. The young ones can be great pests at times, biting, punching, and climbing up and sliding down an adult's body. When an adult has had enough play, it will sometimes lean on the infant until it stops.

Should gorillas be taught sign language?

Koko, a gorilla at the Gorilla Foundation in Woodside, California, has been taught American Sign Language. She knows more than 1,000 signs. Koko can even make jokes with human companions. Some people say this research opens a bridge between gorillas and humans. Others say these studies are a waste.

FOR

1. Gorillas that learn sign language may teach it to other gorillas. This may open new ways of studying how gorillas communicate, think, and feel.
2. Gorillas are intelligent. Language studies may make more people aware of this. More people may then volunteer to help gorillas.

AGAINST

1. Much of what apes like Koko do is imitation or watching their trainers for cues. Gorillas have their own natural communication system. They do not need human sign language.
2. It takes a great deal of time and money to teach gorillas sign language. This money and time could be better used on gorilla conservation.

Guide to Gorillas

Twin gorillas have been born on occasion in zoos. There have been several reports of twins being born in nature, but they did not all survive. Almost all gorilla births are single births.

Young gorillas start to walk when they are 8 or 9 months old. Until then, they cling to their mothers as much as possible.

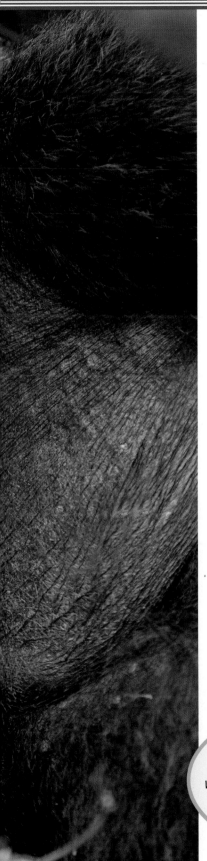

Mating and Birth

The silverback leader mates with most of the adult females in his group. The **gestation period** is 8.5 months. There is no special mating season, so births may happen any month of the year. Most births take place at night, when the group is resting together. Shortly before giving birth, the mother becomes restless and builds a nest. Gorillas generally give birth to one infant at a time. The mother will not give birth again until the youngster is 4 or 5 years old.

Gorilla infants are small and helpless. Their wrinkled faces are pinkish-colored. Their large ears stick out from their heads. An infant's brown eyes are open and curious shortly after birth. Baby gorillas have long, skinny arms and legs. Despite their small size, the infants are quite strong. Their hands and feet can grasp their mother's hair shortly after birth. They can support their weight by one hand for more than three minutes.

Shortly after a gorilla is born, the mother cleans it and puts it on her chest. The infant will nuzzle around and begin to nurse. When morning comes, the other group members will be very interested in the new member. At first, the mother is very protective, but she soon lets the others look at and gently touch her infant. Young gorillas are very important members of the group because they help form social bonds among group members.

From an Expert

"No one who looks into a gorilla's eyes—intelligent, gentle, vulnerable—can remain unchanged, for the gap between ape and human vanishes."
- George Schaller

George Schaller conducted the first in-depth field study of mountain gorillas in 1959. His observations about gorillas have been published in scientific journals and in books, including *The Mountain Gorilla* and *The Year of the Gorilla*. He has also studied and written books about many other endangered species, including African lions, Bengal tigers, and giant pandas.

Baby Gorillas

At birth, gorillas have sparse black hair on their bodies, and they have a tuft of white hair on their rumps. The mother must keep the infant warm until the rest of its hair grows in. A newborn gorilla is also dependent on its mother for nourishment. The mother's milk is the only food it will eat for the first six to eight months. The baby then begins to try different bits of plant food. It learns about different foods by tasting what its mother is eating. An infant gorilla is carried along while the mother feeds.

Between 40 and 50 percent of gorilla infants die while young, despite the fact that gorilla mothers keep their offspring close for up to three years. During the early months of a gorilla's life, its mother is its most important protector and teacher. As the babies get older, other group members also become very important. When a young gorilla is 8 to 12 months old, it will join playgroups of other young gorillas. The large silverback male, usually the father of all the young gorillas in the group, is often tolerant of youngsters. They will play around him or even on him. The silverback is also very protective of the young gorillas, and he keeps a watchful eye on them as they tumble about.

From its pinkish color at birth, a gorilla infant's skin turns to black within two months.

During her lifetime, a female gorilla usually has two or three infants that survive. The babies are born with distinctive noses. As the babies age, their nose prints can be used to tell them apart. Scientists who study gorillas look for how broad and high the nose is, the shape and spacing of the nostrils, and any scars and wrinkles.

The baby gorilla develops at a much faster rate than a human baby does.

Development

The first few years in a gorilla's life are a time to learn many important things, such as what to eat, how to build nests, how to climb trees, and how to avoid danger. The infant will cling to its mother's abdomen, and she will support it with one hand while she moves. At about 7 months of age, infants will ride on their mothers' backs and will eat plants as the majority of their diet.

By the time young gorillas are 12 months of age, hair grows thicker on their bodies, and black hair grows on their heads. Young gorillas continue to nurse while they are learning to eat plants. The young are usually **weaned** by 2 years of age, though some nurse for longer if their mother allows it. During this time, the young gorillas become more independent in every way. By the time they are 2 years old, they are confident enough to follow their group on their own. They will often join in playgroups away from their mother. The white tuft of hair on their rumps disappears by the time they are 4 years old. By this age, they build and sleep in their own nests. They wrestle, climb, and play rowdy games.

BY THE NUMBERS
Although their exact weight varies, healthy gorillas develop in a similar pattern.
Birth   3 to 4 pounds (1.4 to 1.8 kg)
1 Year   15 to 20 pounds (6.8 to 9 kg)
3 Years   60 pounds (27 kg) or so
5 Years   120 pounds (54 kg) or so
8+ Years   150 to 490 pounds (68 to 220 kg), with younger females on the low end and older males on the high end

By 2 years of age, gorillas are able to start gathering their own food.

Take a Stand

Should gorillas be raised in captivity?

Captive gorillas are studied by scientists. The best humanmade habitats have room to roam, trees, and other natural items.

FOR

1. Gorillas have lived 50 years and longer in captivity, which means they do well. What's more, the gorillas in zoos help earn support for gorillas that need help in nature.
2. Most gorillas in zoos are there because they were born there. Their parents were often rescued from situations in which death was certain or likely. Many of these parents were hurt in traps and needed medical attention.

AGAINST

1. The gorillas in zoos tend to weigh more than those in nature. The number-one killer of captive males is heart disease, a by-product of inactivity and unhealthful foods.
2. Captive gorillas lack skills they would have learned in nature. Some captive gorillas are so out of sorts, they are given drugs to keep them calm.

Habitat

Gorillas live in West and Central Africa. Some gorillas live in tropical lowland rainforests, where the temperature can go up to 90° Fahrenheit (32° Celsius). Others live in evergreen mountain forests or dense bamboo forests. Mountain gorillas can be found in forests 11,000 feet (3,350 m) or more above sea level. At that height, temperatures can drop to below freezing at night.

Forest habitats provide gorillas with nesting sites. Gorillas make nests by bending branches and plants into a rough circular shape. Nests vary from about 2 to 5 feet (0.6 to 1.5 m) in diameter. Most gorillas make two nests daily. One is for daytime rest, and the other is for nighttime sleep.

Organizing the Jungle

Earth is home to millions of different **organisms**, all of which have specific survival needs. These organisms rely on their environment, or the place where they live, for their survival. All plants and animals have relationships with their environment. They interact with the environment itself, as well as the other plants and animals within the environment. These interactions create **ecosystems**.

Ecosystems can be broken down into levels of organization. These levels range from a single plant or animal to many species of plants and animals living together in an area.

Organism
A single organism

Population
Many organisms of the same species

Community
Several species living together

Biosphere
Planet Earth and all of its living things

Ecosystem
Many species of plants and animals in an area

Gorillas can be found on the edges of tropical forests and in clearings. They come out of the shade to better enjoy the sunshine.

Range

Gorillas are found mainly along the **equator**, where the forests are warm and support plenty of plant life. There is a variety of lush, green vegetation to eat year-round. The types of plants available to eat can change depending on the season. Gorilla groups travel around their **home range**, or territory, to wherever the best food is growing at the time. A group's home range may be about 5 square miles (13 sq. km) in size. The boundaries of these ranges are flexible. Lowland gorillas usually travel longer distances than mountain gorillas to find the best feeding sites. At higher altitudes, gorillas are able to find more food within a smaller area. Home ranges of different gorilla groups sometimes overlap. If the home ranges of different groups happen to overlap, the animals do not have to fight over food. There are plenty of plants to eat in the rainforest.

Gorillas roam their home ranges during the daylight hours. They rise with the sun and start to search for food. The first feeding lasts for several hours. Then, they rest for two or three hours. They make day nests, which are not as sturdy as the night nests. After resting, the group will travel and feed until late afternoon. At dusk, the group begins to settle down and make nests for the night. The young gorillas sometimes sleep in nests they have made close to their mothers. Male gorillas sometimes share nests with young orphaned gorillas. Their body heat helps keep the young gorillas warm.

Gorillas traveling through their home ranges often use the same trails many times. Observers can tell where gorillas have traveled because they trample a wide path through the dense vegetation. Bent leaves and branches show the direction in which the group has traveled. There may be knuckleprints and footprints in the dirt along the path. These trails often lead to favorite feeding and nesting sites.

Gorilla groups meet and mingle with other groups in their home ranges, but the group members are usually loyal. They return to their original groups afterward.

Guide to Gorillas

The gorillas' search for food and a place to rest determines their range. The gorillas make nests on the ground or even in low trees, depending on their size.

The nest a gorilla makes in daylight tends to be less structured than the nests made at night.

Change in Range

For many years, gorillas lived away from people. The gorillas were secure in their forest homes and sure of their food supply. When loggers began building roads into the forests, the roads opened the gorillas' habitats to settlers and hunters. In the past few decades, the growing human population in Africa's tropical forest regions has forced changes in the gorillas' range and numbers. Some parks and reserves have been set up to try to protect gorillas. Human activity, however, has resulted in the gorillas' decline.

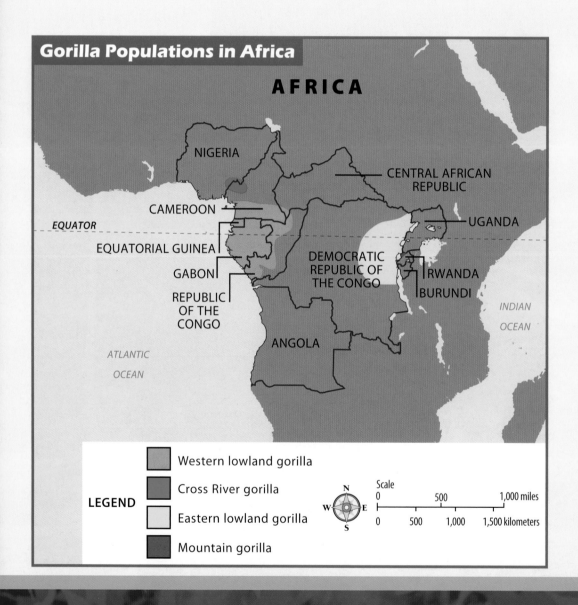

Gorilla Populations in Africa

AFRICA

NIGERIA

CENTRAL AFRICAN REPUBLIC

CAMEROON

UGANDA

EQUATOR

EQUATORIAL GUINEA

GABON

DEMOCRATIC REPUBLIC OF THE CONGO

RWANDA

BURUNDI

REPUBLIC OF THE CONGO

INDIAN OCEAN

ANGOLA

ATLANTIC OCEAN

LEGEND

- Western lowland gorilla
- Cross River gorilla
- Eastern lowland gorilla
- Mountain gorilla

Scale

0   500   1,000 miles

0   500   1,000   1,500 kilometers

N W E S

Civil war broke out in Rwanda in 1990 and lasted for several years. It was a terrible time for the people living in Rwanda. Many thousands of people were killed. Scientists studying gorillas at the Karisoke Research Center, in Rwanda's Volcanoes National Park, had to flee when the fighting spilled into the area. The gorillas managed to survive, although not without problems. When the war ended, the **refugee** camps, filled with hundreds of thousands of people, crowded the edges of the gorillas' habitat in the park. There was a huge demand for firewood and food, and the gorillas' habitat was further damaged. Land mines were left in the park, posing a threat to both people and animals. When the fighting stopped, **poachers**, who had been active in the park before the war, started killing gorillas for profit again.

For better and for worse, the fortunes of the people of Africa and the gorillas remain closely linked. After the war in Rwanda ended, many African trackers and rangers from both of the warring groups joined together to work in the park. They formed anti-poaching and tracking patrols. The patrols look for and destroy traps set by poachers. To track and count the gorillas, the workers count nesting sites and estimate the size of the gorilla groups. The patrols follow the trails of flattened vegetation through the forests in order to collect data. The Karisoke Research Center continues to collect information on the gorillas and their ranges. Researchers look for evidence of illegal activities, and they study ways to make a difference, through medical care and other protections for the gorillas.

Take a Stand

Debate • Research

Should land in Rwanda be set aside for gorilla reserves?

Volcanoes National Park is a 62-square-mile (160-sq.-km) protected area for several hundred mountain gorillas. It is located in the small, poor country of Rwanda.

FOR

1. The gorilla conservation project has brought a great deal of money into the country. Tourism is the country's largest source of foreign cash. Local people get jobs such as guides, wardens, and educators.
2. The people of Rwanda are proud of their role in conserving the rare mountain gorillas. Many people have risked their lives to help protect the gorillas.

AGAINST

1. When the park was formed, land was taken away from some people. These people are no longer allowed to use the land to hunt or herd their animals.
2. People are starving. More people would benefit from growing crops or raising cattle than benefit from gorilla tourism.

Diet

Like many types of plant-eating animals, gorillas spend much of their time looking for plants and eating. Their habitat provides them with a wide variety of food. Some of the gorillas' favorites are wild celery, thistles, nettles, bamboo shoots, blackberries, and ferns. Scientists have discovered that gorillas eat more than 100 different types of plants. Lowland gorillas eat more fruit than mountain gorillas do. There is more fruit available in lowland habitats, although it is found only at certain times and places.

Because of their size, gorillas often stay near the trunk as they climb trees in search of food.

Many of the plants that gorillas like taste bitter to humans. Some of the plants, such as nettles and thistles, have barbs or stinging parts. These do not seem to bother the gorillas. Gorillas often prepare their food by wiping off stinging parts or peeling back outer layers. Gorillas use their hands and teeth to carefully eat different plant parts. They will eat the bark or roots of some plants and the stems, leaves, or berries of others.

Unlike many other animals, gorillas do not seem to search for water to drink. There are not many streams where gorillas live. They seem to get enough water from the dew and rain on the plants. The plants themselves are often juicy and contain moisture.

As herbivores, gorillas leave meat alone. Even if they find a dead animal, they turn away. This does not mean that gorillas avoid all creatures in their diet. Gorillas sometimes eat insects, snails, and slugs on plants. Gorillas have even been observed digging up ant nests and eating the ants inside. When they do this, they must put up with the ants' stings. Not all gorillas will eat ants, but those that do get very excited and even pound on their chests. There have also been reports of gorillas eating honey from beehives. Plants, however, are gorillas' main food. When bamboo shoots are in season, silverbacks can eat as much as 75 pounds (34 kg) each day. When gorillas eat, they usually sit down, with their bellies sticking out between their legs. Gorillas then eat from the plants that are within arm's reach. After eating for several hours, gorillas will rest to digest their food.

Although their large bellies make them look fat, gorillas are actually very strong and muscular. Their bellies store large amounts of bulky vegetation.

The largest part of a gorilla's diet is the leaves, shoots, and stems that it gathers. Gorillas are considered folivores, which means they are herbivores that most often eat leaves.

The Food Cycle

A food cycle shows how energy in the form of food is passed from one living thing to another. As gorillas feed and move through the forest, they affect the lives of the animals around them. The feeding habits of the gorillas produce changes in the environment. In the diagram below, the arrows show the flow of energy from one living thing to another through a **food web**.

Secondary Consumers
Very rarely, a predator such as a leopard will catch and eat a young or very old gorilla. The humans who eat gorilla meat are also in this category of consumers.

Parasites
Gorillas provide a home for parasites such as the hookworm.

Primary Consumers
Gorillas break branches and twigs, drop fruit, and peel strips of vegetation when they feed on plants. This supplies food for smaller creatures, such as ants. As they move through the jungle, gorillas help clear a path for consumers such as the African buffalo.

Producers

The plants in the forest produce food energy from the Sun. Gorillas eat producers such as celery, thistle, and bamboo. Undigested seeds in gorilla droppings help spread plant seeds. This ensures a continuing food supply for gorillas and other animals.

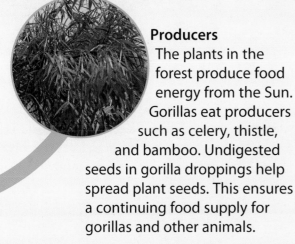

Decomposers

When gorillas die, decomposers break down the gorillas' body materials, adding nutrients to the soil.

Omnivores

Although almost all of their diet is plants, gorillas will sometimes eat ants, ant eggs, or slugs and grubs.

Take a Stand

· Debate ·
· Research ·

Is the work done by patrols that go after poachers worth the risk?

People who cannot afford other meat create a local market for gorilla meat in Africa. In addition, the meat is being exported to other countries, such as Great Britain. This trade is profitable for poachers, who often have few other opportunities for work. The poachers can be violent.

FOR

1. The patrols are an important aspect of government efforts to protect gorillas. Without enforcement, the laws are meaningless.
2. The work of the patrols has led directly to an increase in the number of gorillas in some areas.

AGAINST

1. While saving gorillas is an honorable goal, it is not worth the loss of human life.
2. Creating the protected areas has led to an increase in poachers, because the interest in gorillas has increased and security is inadequate. The patrols should operate only with much more backup.

Guide to Gorillas

In Africa, people with gorilla bites on the buttocks or legs are said to be cowards. This is because when a gorilla runs toward a person, it is usually a bluff charge. If the person stands his or her ground, the gorilla will stop or run past the person. If the person turns and runs, the gorilla will sometimes bite the person's backside.

Though silverbacks sometimes fight to the death, most gorillas try to not kill each other. In most fights, the males bare teeth, slap each other, and turn away.

Competition

In a gorilla group, young gorillas learn how to survive and get along with other gorillas. The group provides gorillas with protection, companions, and playmates. Play is very important to young gorillas. It allows them to test their strength and learn about being a gorilla. Young gorillas usually play in the center of the group, surrounded by adults that protect them. Adults are very good-natured about the youngsters' play. One game is sliding down an adult gorilla's body. Other games that gorillas enjoy are wrestling, tumbling, chasing, and play-fighting.

The rainforest provides a real adventure playground. Young gorillas are excellent tree climbers. They love to swing from low branches and vines. Gorilla observers have called one game "King of the Hill." In this game, young gorillas try to knock one another off a hill or stump. The one who can stay on the hill is the winner. Other games often involve imitating or practicing adult skills. For example, young gorillas break small branches and practice building nests.

Although the gorilla is capable of impressive displays, gorillas are generally calm and tolerant. Gorillas do not need to compete with one another for food. There is usually more than enough for all. At times, there is competition among male gorillas for females. Males within the same group may compete for females, but more often the challenge comes from males outside the group. Young male gorillas spend one stage of their lives on their own, away from their group of origin. They search for females who are willing to join them. Outside challenges come from older males as well. Silverbacks sometimes fight over females. An outsider silverback male may even kill an infant in an attempt to mate with its mother. The group silverback plays a very important role in protecting his young from these and other dangers.

When they are play-fighting, young gorillas learn skills that will come in handy if and when they must actually fight.

Gorillas with Other Animals

Gorillas share their habitat with many animals. These animals can include elephants, small antelope, buffalo, monkeys, and chimpanzees. In almost all cases, the gorillas go about their business and let the other animals go about theirs. Some of the other animals eat the same kinds of plants as gorillas. There are plenty of plants, however, so this is not usually a problem. Even when two animals eat the same kind of plant, they do not always eat the same parts. For example, gorillas and buffalo both like to eat nettles. Buffalo nip off the tender tops, while gorillas like the roots, stems, and leaves.

Some animals use gorilla trails to help them get around. Buffalo will follow gorilla groups closely as they travel through the dense plants. Gorillas sometimes bluff charge the buffalo. It has been observed that gorillas seem to enjoy scattering the buffalo in all directions.

It seems that gorillas have only one serious competitor. The most trouble that gorillas face comes directly from human beings. People compete for the gorillas' habitat, and they kill gorillas for food and profit. Large numbers of people live and farm in parts of Africa where gorillas live. The number of people who affect the gorillas keeps growing. Some people destroy the forest by running their cattle through it. In countries where wood is the only fuel for warmth and cooking, the forest trees are in great demand. In some areas, the gorillas themselves are regularly hunted and eaten. Africans also hunt gorillas when gorillas eat their crops.

Forest buffalo live in the tropical forests of West and Central Africa. These large creatures have tempers and have been known to annoy the gorillas in their midst.

Guide to Gorillas

Chimpanzees are the only apes that will hunt and regularly eat meat. Even when they share a gorilla's habitat, they do not compete for food. There have been cases of leopards that have attacked and killed gorillas, but few predators, except for humans, risk attacking an adult gorilla.

Gorillas are affected by many of the same diseases that hurt humans. The tourists who view gorillas are asked to stay home if they are sick with illnesses that are catching, such as pneumonia.

Folklore

African stories describe fierce battles between gorillas and leopards. The gorilla often defeats the leopard by swinging it until the leopard's tail comes off. In one legend of the Bulu tribe in West Africa, the gorilla is a brother of humans. God gave all of his children fire, seeds, and tools. As the gorilla moved through the forest, it stopped to eat some fruit. By the time it had finished eating, its fire was out. God said that because of this, gorillas would have to live in the forest forever, and they would always have to flee from humans.

Gorillas have long captured human imagination. Animals like gorillas are mentioned in Roman documents that are 2,500 years old. In the mid-1800s and after, numerous expeditions were sent to Africa from Europe and North America to shoot or capture these mysterious animals. Gorilla specimens were put on exhibit, which raised curiosity among people.

In the 1900s, storytellers invented the character King Kong. In a story that was made into movies, Kong lives on an island with prehistoric creatures. A team of hunters captures him and brings him to the United States so they can place him in an exhibit. Kong manages to escape, but he is killed by fighter planes as he climbs the Empire State Building in New York City. Most movies portray gorillas as dangerous or stupid. It is only in the past few decades that people have begun to look beyond the gorilla's appearance and have begun to understand its behavior.

The original *King Kong* movie was released in 1933. There have been several remakes.

Myth	**VS**	Fact

Gorillas are ferocious and dangerous animals. They will attack and kill humans.

Gorillas are peaceful, gentle animals. They will, however, fight to protect themselves and their group. The silverbacks are particularly protective of the young in their groups. When gorillas have bitten or injured humans, they were usually acting in self-defense or protecting their young.

When gorillas pound their chests, it means they are angry and will attack you.

All gorillas, including infants, slap their chests. It can be an impressive display that often ends in a bluff charge rather than an actual attack. It can also be done in play, to show off, or to relieve stress.

The gorilla is a slow, lazy animal that spends most of its time sitting and eating.

Gorillas must spend a great deal of time eating. However, they are always alert to their environment, and they can move very quickly if danger threatens.

In 2005, a replica of a giant gorilla appeared in Times Square in New York City. It was part of the promotion for a more recent version of the film *King Kong*, which was directed by Peter Jackson.

Status

Gorilla populations are declining for several reasons. Two of the worst problems facing gorillas are habitat loss and poaching. The gorilla's forest home has always provided for all of its needs. Pressure from humans, however, is now causing gorilla habitats to shrink. People want to cut down forests to get lumber or to make room for farms and mines.

Many acres of trees are cut down to make room for mines and the roads leading to them. Coltan is a kind of mineral that is used to make cell phone circuits. The mineral is rare worldwide but is found in some parts of Africa. About 80 percent of the world's supply is being mined in the Democratic Republic of the Congo, in Central Africa. Mining companies are taking over land that used to be gorilla habitat. This forces the gorillas into impossible situations. Gorillas will not go very far into open woodlands or grasslands. They cannot swim, so streams and rivers form another habitat boundary. When rainforests are destroyed, gorillas are trapped in small pockets of forest. They can no longer wander freely. As farms appear closer to their homes, gorillas may raid crops and come into conflict with people. This leads to additional gorilla deaths.

All gorilla populations are declining because of poaching. Some gorillas get free from poachers' snares and recover, but others die from their injuries or are permanently maimed. Some gorillas end up with missing or deformed fingers, hands, or feet because of snares. In the lowlands of Africa, large numbers of gorillas are being killed for food. Much of this food feeds the work crews who are cutting down the forests. The miners who travel into the forest to search for coltan eat gorillas, because there are few other food sources available. The meat is also sold in African markets. Dogs are often used to track and hunt down gorillas. The hands and heads of gorillas are sold by poachers. They are used as charms by local people or are bought as souvenirs by tourists.

The gorillas in the Bwindi Impenetrable Forest in Uganda are the subject of intense study by scientists.

Civil wars and political unrest among humans have also taken a toll on gorillas who live in affected areas.

Half of the world's population of mountain gorillas lives within the Bwindi Impenetrable Forest. Some of their forest home is within a national park.

One of the threats to the gorillas is the sale of their young to people who wish to own exotic animals.

Animals on the Brink

Saving the Gorilla

Various governments and other groups are doing what they can to save the gorilla. Both species of gorilla have been classified as endangered. This means that the animals are in danger of not surviving. Gorillas are protected under an international agreement called the Convention on International Trade in Endangered Species of Wild Fauna and Flora (CITES). Since 1973, the nations that have signed CITES have agreed to laws that stop the trade of endangered animals or their parts. In the year 2000, the United States passed legislation that sets aside money to help save gorillas and other apes.

In Africa, there are eight nations with laws to protect gorillas from poachers or other hunters. In some areas, such as Volcanoes National Park in Rwanda, anti-poaching patrols destroy poachers' snares and arrest any poachers they can find. Because they must cover large areas, the patrols cannot stop all poaching, but the efforts of the patrols have saved some of the gorillas.

Conservation efforts in poor countries work only if local people will benefit from the conservation. To address this fact of life, Rwanda has created a tourism industry around the gorilla. Many foreigners will pay a great deal of money to see gorillas in their natural habitat. The tourism program is built around the desire to protect the gorillas. Related programs help make it attractive to save forests and to use products from the forest in a way that promotes the continued growth of this habitat.

Rwanda's currency now features a picture of the gorilla, showing the animal's importance to the country's economy. Education and public awareness are key to protection of the animals. Some programs try to get the word out that eating bushmeat increases the dangers of certain kinds of disease. Other programs search for alternatives for coltan.

From an Expert

Dian Fossey studied mountain gorillas in Rwanda from 1966 until 1985. She set up the Karisoke Research Center to study gorillas, and she uncovered many new facts about gorilla society. Fossey published several articles and a book, *Gorillas in the Mist*, about her work with gorillas.

"...en you realize the value of all life, you ...d less on what is past and concentrate ...re on the preservation of the future."
- Dian Fossey

Back from the Brink

Gorillas are at risk wherever they live in nature. They are endangered due to habitat destruction, disease, and hunting. Just 700 or so mountain gorillas are left. Eastern lowland gorillas are now limited to the eastern Democratic Republic of the Congo. Though western lowland gorillas number about 150,000 throughout West and Central Africa, they are dying rapidly from disease caused by the Ebola virus.

Civil war in Rwanda interrupted gorilla rescue efforts in the 1990s. In 2007, gorillas in the Democratic Republic of the Congo came under threat when war erupted there. The gorillas have survived against great odds, but they still need support from organizations that try to save them. One such organization is the Dian Fossey Gorilla Fund. Dian Fossey was a researcher who studied mountain gorillas in Rwanda. In 1977, one of her favorite gorillas, Digit, was killed while defending his group from poachers. As a result, Fossey started a successful fund to protect gorillas. In 1985, there were fewer than 250 gorillas in the Rwanda mountains. As of 2012, there were nearly 500.

For more information on the gorilla rescue program, contact:

Dian Fossey Gorilla Fund International
800 Cherokee Avenue, S.E.
Atlanta, GA 30315

Researchers estimate that the population of the western lowland gorilla has been reduced by 80 percent or more in the past three generations.

Activity

Debating helps people think about ideas thoughtfully and carefully. When people debate, two sides take a different viewpoint on a subject. Each side takes turns presenting arguments to support its view.

Use the Take a Stand sections found throughout this book as a starting point for debate topics. Organize your friends or classmates into two teams. One team will argue in favor of the topic, and the other will argue against. Each team should research the issue thoroughly using reliable sources of information, including books, scientific journals, and trustworthy websites. Take notes of important facts that support your side of the debate. Prepare your argument using these facts to support your opinion.

During the debate, the members of each team are given a set amount of time to make their arguments. The team arguing the For side goes first. They have five minutes to present their case. All members of the team should participate equally. Then, the team arguing the Against side presents its arguments. Each team should take notes of the main points the other team argues.

After both teams have made their arguments, they get three minutes to prepare their **rebuttals**. Teams review their notes from the previous round. The teams focus on trying to disprove each of the main points made by the other team using solid facts. Each team gets three minutes to make its rebuttal. The team arguing the Against side goes first. Students and teachers watching the debate serve as judges. They should try to judge the debate fairly using a standard score sheet, such as the example below.

Criteria	Rate: 1-10	Sample Comments
1. Were the arguments well organized?	8	logical arguments, easy to follow
2. Did team members participate equally?	9	divided time evenly between members
3. Did team members speak loudly and clearly?	3	some members were difficult to hear
4. Were rebuttals specific to the other team's arguments?	6	rebuttals were specific, more facts needed
5. Was respect shown for the other team?	10	all members showed respect to the other team

Quiz

1. What are mature male gorillas called?

2. To which order of animals do gorillas belong?

3. Which subspecies of gorilla is the most widespread?

4. What is the name for the bony ridge on the top of a gorilla's head?

5. What does it mean when a gorilla belches?

6. Which language has Koko the gorilla been taught?

7. How often does a gorilla make a nest?

9. What interrupted gorilla rescue efforts in Rwanda in the 1990s?

8. What do gorillas most like to eat?

10. What feature can be used to identify gorillas?

Key Words

canine: a pointed tooth

ecosystems: communities of living things and resources

equator: an imaginary line around the center of Earth, dividing the northern and southern hemispheres

family: one of eight major ranks used to classify animals, between order and genus

food web: connecting food chains that show how energy flows from one organism to another through diet

genetic evidence: the results of tests that examine genes, the building blocks for making living things, to discover the origin or development of a species

gestation period: the length of time that a female is pregnant

herbivore: an animal that prefers to eat plants

home range: the entire area in which a gorilla group lives

knuckle-walking: movement in which a gorilla's feet are flat on the ground and most of its body weight is carried on its knuckles

opposable: the ability to place either the first finger and thumb or the big and second toes together to grasp objects

order: one of eight major ranks used to classify animals, between class and family

organisms: forms of life

poachers: people who kill an animal illegally

primates: a large category of animals that includes prosimians, monkeys, apes, and humans

rebuttals: attempts to counter, or disprove, an argument

refugee: a person who flees his or her homeland to escape war, persecution, or violence

sagittal crest: large, bony crest at the top of a gorilla's head to which its jaw muscles are attached

species: groups of individuals with common characteristics

vocalizations: sounds made to send messages to others or that express emotions

weaned: when a young gorilla does not drink milk from its mother anymore

Index

Log on to www.av2books.com

AV² by Weigl brings you media enhanced books that support active learning. Go to www.av2books.com, and enter the special code found on page 2 of this book. You will gain access to enriched and enhanced content that supplements and complements this book. Content includes video, audio, weblinks, quizzes, a slide show, and activities.

Audio
Listen to sections of the book read aloud.

Video
Watch informative video clips.

Embedded Weblinks
Gain additional information for research.

Try This!
Complete activities and hands-on experiments.

WHAT'S ONLINE?

Try This!	Embedded Weblinks	Video	EXTRA FEATURES
Chart the levels of organization within the biosphere.	Learn more about gorillas.	Watch a video about gorillas.	**Audio** Listen to sections of the book read aloud.
Map gorilla habitats around the world.	Read about gorilla conservation efforts.	See gorillas in their natural habitat.	
Complete a food web for gorillas.	Find out more about gorilla habitats.		**Key Words** Study vocabulary, and complete a matching word activity.
Label and describe the parts of the gorilla.	Discover more fascinating facts about gorillas.		**Slide Show** View images and caption and prepare a presentati
Classify gorillas using a classification diagram.	Learn more about what you can do to help save gorillas.		**Quizzes** Test your knowledge.

AV² was built to bridge the gap between print and digital. We encourage you to tell us what you like and what you want to see in the future.

Sign up to be an AV² Ambassador at www.av2books.com/ambassador.